To Serve and Protect

Copyright © 2022 Perpetual Light Publishing. All rights reserved. No part of this book may be reproduced by any means without the written permission of the author and/or publisher.

First Edition: April 2022
ISBN 978-1-7356643-9-2

Special thanks to Tressa Lindsay at Bird's-eye Edits.

www.perpetuallightpublishing.com

I will always protect you from danger at home.

And while away.

Operation search and rescue.

I will never leave a fallen family member.

"I'm home!"

Written by
Leslea Wahl

This is me and my mom. We live in Colorado where I work really hard to keep my family safe from the perils of the world. Mom is an author, so she gets to spend a lot of time at home with me. Although I sometimes wish she'd spend less time on her computer so we could play more often.

Having a mom who is an author has its benefits. Besides writing about me in this picture book, she has also made me a character in one of her teen novels. You can find more about us at

www.LesleaWahl.com.

Illustrated by Amy Klein

This is my fairy dog-mother who gave me my colorful name! Art is her passion. She loves to illustrate books, paint murals, design toys, and decorate cakes. This is the fourth children's book she has illustrated and is thrilled to work with her friend, my mom, Leslea.

She loves the outdoors and is inspired by nature while hiking, skiing, paddle boarding, and soaking up the Colorado sunshine. See her work at

www.amykleindesign.com.

Authors depend upon

BOOK REVIEWS!

We can't continue our work without your help. If you've enjoyed this story, please leave a few words on your favorite BOOK-REVIEW platform.

www.perpetuallightpublishing.com

Made in the USA
Middletown, DE
09 November 2023